THE GOLF CODE

A GUIDE TO LIFE THROUGH THE EYES OF GOLF

BEST-SELLING AUTHOR
GEORGE BAKRNCHEV, BBSC. (PSYCH.)
DOUBLE MAJOR IN HUMAN APPLIED PSYCHOLOGY

Thank you, Dad!

I still remember the first time you took me to play golf.

As a primary school kid, all I could recall was how long it took to finish.

But that experience was enough to get me to play it again many, many years later.

You planted the seed for an incurable zest to play the greatest game on Earth and to unlock the life lessons that lie within it.

Copyright © 2024 by George Bakrnchev
All rights reserved.

No part of this book may be reproduced in any form or by any electronic or mechanical means, including information storage and retrieval systems, without written permission from the author, except for the use of brief quotations in a book review.

Paperback ISBN: 978-0-9804456-8-8
Hardcover ISBN: 978-0-9804456-9-5
eBook ISBN: 978-0-9925142-0-4

START HERE

Pick a page number between 2 and 264

Write it down here:_____

Now turn to that page and take note of the chapter title.

You have just chosen your first lesson out of the book.
Enjoy the transformation

CONTENTS

Introduction x
Perfection 2
Gratefulness 4
The Three S's 6
Power Of Now 8
Your Brain's Filter 10
Stuff Ups 12
The Feel 14
The Starting Point 16
Belief 18
The Jitters 20
Fear 22
The Scorecard 24
Results Vs. Activities 26
Progress 28
Friends 30
Practice 32
Knowing Isn't Enough 34
The Two C's 36
Switching Off 38
Multi-Tasking 40
Losing 42
Overthinking 44

Control	46
Be Present	48
Discipline	50
Falling Short	52
Poor Start	54
Humble	56
Expectations	58
The Journey	60
Honesty	62
Right Approach	64
Skills	66
Implementation	68
Perception	70
Tired	72
Nerves	74
Work & Life	76
Stuck	78
Information	80
Effortless	82
Hard Vs. Solid	84
Efficient Vs. Effective	86
Resilience	88
Grateful	90
Taking It For Granted	92
Two Words	94
Balance	96

Seize The Moment	98
Anxiety	100
Persistence	102
Self-Interest	104
Acceptance	106
The Caddie	108
Stuff-Less	110
Problems	112
Reliable	114
It Is Written	116
Curiosity	118
Value	120
Reflection	122
Indecisive	124
Wins Vs. Losses	126
Your Actions	128
The Shop Front	130
Adapt	132
Unexpected	134
Overwhelm	136
In The Now	138
Behavior	140
Up & Down	142
Change	144
Life	146
Being On A High	148

Remember The Good	150
Coaches	152
Judgement	154
Good Luck Vs. Bad Luck	156
Percentage	158
The Cup	160
Recovery	162
Unsure	164
Outsiders	166
Logic	168
Saying Sorry	170
Why Am I Doing This?	172
High Risk - High Reward?	174
Negative Spiral	176
Serious People	178
Focus	180
Unconscious Effort	182
Dealing With Failure	184
Money	186
Personality	188
Worry	190
Stress	192
Unique Teamwork	194
Doubt	196
It Is What It Is	198
Perfect Timing	200

Appreciation 202
Positive Thinking 204
Play It For Me 206
Motivation 208
Failure 210
Staying Small 212
Negative Patterns 214
Slow Down To Speed Up 216
The Comparison Trap 218
Superstitions 220
External Environment 222
Internal Environment 224
Emotional Intelligence 226
People Change 228
Opinions 230
Hazards 232
True Costs 234
Success 236
Anger 238
Choices 240
Degree Of Difficulty 242
Food Swings 244
Importance 246
Wrong Environment 248
Rewire Your Brain 250
Strengths Vs. Weaknesses 252

The Smallest Club	254
Big Rewards	256
A Full Mind	258
One Small Divot	260
Technical Vs. Strategic	262
The Last Round	264

INTRODUCTION

WHY GOLF?

I took up golf as an escape.

I needed to get away from modern technologies and modern distractions.

I needed a way to clear my mind, a way to let my thoughts take a rest, a way to get back to nature, to be surrounded by water, exotic birds, wildlife, trees, and greenery that would spoil my eyes and mind.

Little did I know that golf would provide me with far more than I ever thought possible.

The unique lens of golf gave me answers and explained life in the most fascinating way.

Legendary golfers have referred to golf as being a 'spiritual' experience.

There just isn't another game like it. It's a game where the lowest score wins and the actual lowest score possible will never be achieved… EVER.

Unlike a football field, which is fixed in size and every player knows the boundaries, with golf, no two courses are ever the same.

In fact, the course you play on right now will be different in a few minutes' time.

They say you 'drive for show' and 'putt for dough'.

The putting green is typically where fame and fortunes are either won or lost.

Yet it has the most unstable playing surface in any game.

It is in a constant state of change, and you are expected to master it if you are serious about the game.

The putting surface changes according to the wind, the moisture in the air, the amount of sunshine it soaks in, the amount of shadow it has on it, how fast the grass blades grow, and even how many players have walked on it prior to you.

It's an extraordinarily difficult game to master and that's the addiction.

It is a game of highs and lows, as is life. You have to continually adjust yourself to external conditions and how you are feeling, both physically and emotionally.

The game of golf doesn't care about your looks, your religion, your caste, your wealth, your fears, your doubts, your strengths, or your weaknesses.

It doesn't care if you are good or bad, who your parents are, what you do, where you've been, or what you have or have not done in life. It simply does not care… it's not relevant!

The game of golf does not judge. It does not discriminate.

It says, 'Here I am. Play me as you wish. Your skills, thoughts, and actions will determine your results." Full stop!

It's when I realized this that I started to see how golf, of all activities, has the profound ability to transform your emotions and your behaviors for the better.

My sincerest wish is that *The Golf Code* will unlock the perspective and skills you need in order to better understand how to do this thing called life.

George Bakrnchev

George Bakrnchev, BBSc.

Double Major in Human Applied Psychology,
Best-Selling Author, Resilient Golfer

*Golf is the closest game to
the game we call life*

- Bobby Jones

PERFECTION

In GOLF:

What is a perfect score in golf?

72, 71, 59, 54?

It's actually 18.

18 holes-in-one.

I did say 'perfect' score.

Are you ever going to achieve this perfect score?

No.

Will anyone achieve this level of perfection?

No.

Does it stop any of us from playing the game?

No.

Golf is naturally a game of progress.

It will never be perfected because that is not the aim of the game.

PERFECTION

In LIFE:

As in golf, you don't need to be perfect to do extremely well.

But you do need to progress to do extremely well.

Make progress your daily goal, not perfection.

Set progress goals in all areas of your life.

Relationships… set progress goals.

Finances… set progress goals.

Health… set progress goals.

The instant you adopt a progressive mindset, you will notice a huge weight being lifted off your shoulders.

The quality and enjoyment of your life will also change forever. Your ability to achieve will also accelerate.

Aim for progress, not perfection.

Be progressive.

GRATEFULNESS

In GOLF:

You wake up, you turn up, and you play the game.

Reflect for a moment, and think about everything that makes it possible for you to do that.

That is you being grateful.

It's the easiest thing you can do, and the thing you do least.

GRATEFULNESS

In LIFE:

Being able to wake up and show up in life is a monumental feat and privilege.

So many things have to go right for you to be able to do that.

Sit still for a full minute and run through all the things that went right for you up until this point to enable you to do what you're about to do.

Those are the things you can start being most grateful for.

Everything else that happens after that minute of reflection is a bonus.

Don't rely on getting energy from things outside of yourself to make you happy.

When you are grateful, you create an energy within yourself to live happier.

Be grateful that you can be grateful.

THE THREE S'S

In GOLF:

You wake up all fired up about your upcoming round… today is going to be YOUR day.

Then, by the end of the round, reality hits you. You've just posted one of your worst rounds ever.

Is this cause to feel down, even depressed?

Or was it a great day of feedback?

Beware of the perspective you choose.

Here's a winner's perspective:

Every golfer's success story follows the three S's: Stretch, Struggle, Success.

None of them achieved success without going through the stretch and struggle first.

THE THREE S'S

In LIFE:

You weren't born to achieve happiness.

You were born to be resilient.

You were born to face and endure setbacks, mishaps, errors, joy, and elation.

That is how you grow.

Through stretch and struggle, you achieve success.

Just watch a toddler try to stand for the first time.

They fall over and over again, and even hurt themselves in the process, but they don't give up.

They instinctively stretch and struggle to get to success.

Look forward to the stretch and struggle.

Reset your perspective. Your experiences are getting you one step closer to success.

The bigger your stretch and struggle, the bigger your success.

Be resilient.

POWER OF NOW

In GOLF:

There's the past, the future, and the now

Try playing 'future' golf or 'past' golf… it's a pointless exercise

The only effective golf is 'now' golf.

POWER OF NOW

In LIFE:

Life might seem like you have a past or a future, but in reality, neither the past nor the future exist.

So, what's left, and where's your real power?

Your real power is in the 'Micro-Now's'.

Right now is the most powerful moment you'll ever have in your life.

Be aware of what you're doing in each 'micro-now'.

Each one will fall effortlessly into the next one, creating a domino effect of 'micro-now's'.

These will, eventually, become your life—not yesterday, not tomorrow, but now.

YOUR BRAIN'S FILTER

In GOLF:

Let's say you start to 'think' about buying a new putter.

Almost like magic, you will start to see that putter model everywhere (and I'm not talking about social media re-targeting).

Yet, before you decided on that specific putter, you probably didn't see it at all.

So, what happened to your brain here?

You just activated your RAS: your Reticular Activating System.

Think of your RAS as a kind of gatekeeper for your brain.

It filters a massive amount of information that your brain receives every micro-second, and it instantly decides what information to filter IN and what information to filter OUT based on what you thought about—in this case, a particular brand of putter.

YOUR BRAIN'S FILTER

In LIFE:

You see what you want to see. That's how your RAS works

It's up to you to filter IN what's important to you and filter OUT what's not.

This is why goal setting is so powerful.

When you write down a goal, you are informing your RAS in a really important way, reminding it that this is what you need to filter IN.

Then, all of a sudden, the right people and the right events will start to appear to help you achieve your goal.

Write it down.

STUFF UPS

In GOLF:

What is the most important thing to do when you stuff up a shot?

You recover.

STUFF UPS

In LIFE:

Focus on the steps you need to take right now in order to set up a path of recovery.

Recovering from a bad situation can be more rewarding and more impactful on your senses than when things automatically go well.

We all love a great recovery story, and that story all begins with a stuff up.

See your stuff ups as your opportunity in disguise.

THE FEEL

In GOLF:

Should you cut the corner and go over the water or lay up?

The answer lies in the 'feel' response you get when you ask yourself that question.

Don't answer it with a brain response. Instead, answer this question with a 'whole body' response.

Your brain only thinks, and that's part of the solution, but golf requires a whole solution.

Your whole body feels the whole situation.

THE FEEL

In LIFE:

What do you do when you are faced with a situation that you have never been in before?

What do you do when you're not sure what action to take?

Go for the whole-body feel, not just what you 'think'.

Every cell in your body has intelligence, not just the brain.

Go for what you think AND feel as a whole body.

Then, commit to your course of action without ANY doubt.

Answer questions with your whole-body feel.

THE STARTING POINT

In GOLF:

Why do the tee off boxes have markers?

The markers give you a starting point. They are where the action starts.

Without them, chaos would rule, and the game would not work.

THE STARTING POINT

In LIFE:

Everything you do in life has 3 stages to it.

The start.

The middle.

The end.

Nothing happens until you start.

Be a starter.

BELIEF

In GOLF:

When you say to yourself that you will win today, that is your belief in action.

One slip of your belief, and your whole outcome changes.

Re-align your belief, and your whole outcome changes again.

If you are fickle with your belief, so, too, will be your scorecard.

BELIEF

In LIFE:

There are two types of belief.

Internal Belief—a belief from within you that moves you.

External Belief—a belief from outsiders that moves you.

I can give you my belief of you to help you drive forward in your life (that's external belief), but I can't make you believe that you can do it (that's internal belief).

Talk will only get you so far. Ultimately, only you can take the necessary action to move forward.

To take action, you must believe that you can perform, even beyond what you thought possible.

Belief is your x-factor that produces magic.

THE JITTERS

In GOLF:

It's the first tee, all eyes are on you, and all of a sudden, you get the jitters.

The jitters come from feeling the expectation of the moment.

Drop your expectation, and a calmness will take over.

A calm, mentally powerful player is really something to behold.

THE JITTERS

In LIFE:

It's not how you start but how you finish that matters.

But you will need to start in order to finish.

The only expectation is the expectation you place on yourself.

This can be paralysing.

The jitters are normal when you start anything.

Let's reframe your jitters.

'What a privilege it is to be here. Let's begin the journey.'

Goodbye, jitters.

FEAR

In GOLF:

Two of you are looking at the exact same hole at the exact same time.

Yet one of you feels fear, and the other feels excitement.

So, whose feelings are correct?

FEAR

In LIFE:

If one of you feels fear and the other feels excitement over the exact same event, then neither of you are wrong nor right!

The reality of the event is the same for both of you.

It's your reaction to that reality that determines how you feel.

Your feelings are 'imagined' to be true. They are not right or wrong.

The key is to decide which response will motivate you to give you the best outcome.

Motivate your fear.

THE SCORECARD

In GOLF:

For your round to count in competitive golf, you must hand in a correctly filled-in scorecard.

THE SCORECARD

In LIFE:

Your scorecard in life is filled by the things you did or did not do.

Do what you need to do.

RESULTS VS. ACTIVITIES

In GOLF:

You write down your score after every hole. That's your 'result'.

A result is a result. It's not changeable.

The actions that led to your result are changeable.

Improvement comes from working on the activity, not the result.

RESULTS VS. ACTIVITIES

In LIFE:

A result doesn't just appear.

Every result has a string of 'activities' that has led to it.

If you are serious about changing your results, look at the activities that led to that result.

Your current situation, your current lifestyle that you enjoy or don't enjoy, is a direct reflection of your thoughts and the actions you took or didn't take.

It's too easy to blame the past or another person, but deep down, you know that's just a cop out for not taking responsibility.

By all means, have a picture of the result you want.

But, instead of focusing on the result, focus on the activities, the thoughts and actions, that will give you that result.

The right activities will give you the right results.

Choose the right activities.

PROGRESS

In GOLF:

You don't start golf today and become a scratch player tomorrow.

There is no overnight success.

And there is no perfect.

There is only progress.

PROGRESS

In LIFE:

Once you accept that there is no perfection, only progress, your whole energy will shift to accelerate your progress.

How do you accelerate your progress?

Focus on being these two things:

Constant and consistent in your thoughts.

Constant and consistent in your actions.

While doing this, aim for progress, not perfection, in your thoughts and actions.

Progress rules!

FRIENDS

In GOLF:

The maximum number of players allowed in any grouping is four.

If you have good golfing friends, you are lucky.

If you're playing alone, you'll be paired up with other players you may have never met before.

By going out to play on your own, you instantly increase your chances of making new friends based around one common desire—to play golf.

FRIENDS

In LIFE:

If you have three close friends that can be there for you during the ups and downs of life, you are blessed.

It's up to you to find those friends.

Your friends will play different roles for you in many ways, but there will always be a commonality that binds you all.

Cherish the friends that bring out the best in you.

PRACTICE

In GOLF:

There's practice, and then there's deliberate practice.

You can go out and practice by hitting 100 chip shots.

Or you can go out and practice 100 chip shots with the focus of landing 80% of them within 10ft / 3m of the target.

That's deliberate practice!

That's the difference between becoming good or becoming great.

PRACTICE

In LIFE:

It's too easy to amble along life, doing the same old same old, day in, day out.

But does it bring you the results you really want?

When you stop just 'doing' and start focusing your actions with a deliberate goal in mind, you will be amazed at the changes you see in your life.

Be deliberate and specific about your health, your relationships, and your career.

Try this:

Pick a deliberate and specific goal for your health.

Let's say your goal is to halve the quantity of what you eat at each meal in order to lose weight.

Do this every day for 21 days.

Watch the weight drop off.

Be deliberate.

KNOWING ISN'T ENOUGH

In GOLF:

Watching golf improvement videos is pointless unless you go out and put those ideas into physical practice.

Until then, all you have is a mind full of fanciful ideas.

There's a big gap between knowing and doing.

KNOWING ISN'T ENOUGH

In LIFE:

There is an old saying: 'To know and not do is not yet to know'.

In other words, knowledge is not enough.

You must 'do'.

Only then will you truly begin to understand what that knowledge means.

Stop saying 'I know', and start saying 'I am doing'.

THE TWO C'S

In GOLF:

It takes time, a LOT of time, to become great at golf.

The foundations to becoming a great player are not as exciting as the media might portray.

Greatness involves the two 'C's'.

You must be CONSTANT and CONSISTENT.

And you must be this way over many, many years with both your thoughts and your actions.

This is the true secret to success.

Yes, it will feel boring and repetitive.

And that's why only a small number of golfers will ever become great.

THE TWO C'S

In LIFE:

Pick any goal that you're passionate about, and apply the two 'C's' to it.

Take weight loss as an example.

Design a CONSTANT and CONSISTENT weight loss program, and support it with your thoughts and actions.

Take investing as another.

Design a CONSTANT and CONSISTENT investment program, and support it with your thoughts and actions.

Take loving relationships as one more.

Design CONSTANT and CONSISTENT loving relationship behavior, and support it with your thoughts and your actions.

Figure out what you desire, and then commit to being CONSTANT and CONSISTENT in both your thoughts and your actions.

Love the two C's.

SWITCHING OFF

In GOLF:

There are a lot of distractions when playing golf.

You have external distractions: your playing environment, the weather, the course conditions, your playing partners, etc.

You have internal distractions: your anxiety levels, your confidence levels, your aches and pains, your hunger levels, your work stresses, relationship stresses, etc.

If you could only switch off those distractions, you'd play better golf, right?

Wrong. Read on…

SWITCHING OFF

In LIFE:

Your mind is not capable of switching off.

The key is to switch ON your mind to ONE thing—and one thing only.

By doing this, you will automatically switch everything else OFF for that moment.

This will make you hyper-focused on that one thing.

And when you are focused on that one thing, you will begin to produce magical results.

Switch ON one thing in order to switch OFF everything else in your life.

Switch on your magic.

MULTI-TASKING

In GOLF:

Imagine trying to putt and drive the ball at the same time… that's multi-tasking.

You would never do it, and there's a very good reason why.

You would produce a terrible score.

You drive the ball, and then you putt the ball.

This is called 'task-switching'.

Task-switching is how you produce your best scores.

MULTI-TASKING

In LIFE:

Multi-tasking doesn't work.

When you are truly 'in the now', there are no noises, no distractions.

Many things are fighting for your attention.

It is impossible to be totally focused on two things at once.

So, decide what's important for you to do right now.

Trust that devoted focus and see it through.

Your results by following a singular focus will be outstanding.

Do one task to your highest ability, then switch to the next task to your highest ability.

That's the art of single-task switching.

Break down all goals, big or small, into single tasks.

Multi-tasking doesn't work. Single-tasking does.

LOSING

In GOLF:

The game of golf is designed to produce winners and losers.

Statistics show that you will lose a lot more than you will ever win.

Sure, you go into a tournament to win, but the statistics are against you.

Yet, you still go out and play this great game—and so you should.

The world's best players ALWAYS lose more than they win, yet they are still known as the best players in the world.

LOSING

In LIFE:

The secret is not to look at losing as losing.

Losing is life's way of providing you with feedback.

Feedback is essential to your journey of progress.

You don't lose… you progress in life.

Life is full of wins and losses. It's the contrast between the two that gives it beauty.

The more you lose, the more you win.

OVERTHINKING

In GOLF:

Golf is hard enough to play with a clear mind, let alone with a cluttered mind.

Too many golfers turn up to the first tee with their mind full of 'stuff'.

That stuff will make its way to your scorecard, and it won't be pretty.

OVERTHINKING

In LIFE:

Your aim is to become 'stuff-less'.

Practice this simple mantra: trust, let go, enjoy.

Say this before any major action you take.

This will put you into a relaxed, hyper-focused, clear-thinking state to help you do your best with what you have in front of you.

Enjoy being 'stuff-less'.

CONTROL

In GOLF:

There are so many factors that will determine how well you play each day.

The weather, the course conditions, the people in your playing group, just to name a few, will all be a factor in how you score.

All these things are out of your control, yet we crave to control our game's outcome.

CONTROL

In LIFE:

You can only control the controllables.

So, what's controllable?

Your emotions, your reactions, your strategy, what you eat and drink, these are all 'within' you.

You have total control over all of them.

Accept the uncontrollable.

And control the controllables.

BE PRESENT

In GOLF:

How well would you play if your mind was elsewhere?

When you are totally present, totally in the moment, you don't see or hear anything other than what's in front of you.

When you are in this mode, you can't be rattled.

This is a crucial element of success.

You have become unshakable in that moment.

BE PRESENT

In LIFE:

To be 'present', you will need to be 'absent' from everything else.

You become present when you only have one thing to focus on.

There is a time and place for everything, but the present moment is reserved for that one 'something'.

This is where the magic happens for you.

When you only have one thing to focus on, the amount of energy and focus you can devote to that one thing will be truly amazing—and so, too, will your outcome.

The present is the most valuable gift you can give yourself.

Accept gifts.

DISCIPLINE

In GOLF:

I've got news for you.

Playing great golf has nothing, and I mean NOTHING, to do with your discipline.

Let me explain…

DISCIPLINE

In LIFE:

Have you ever said to yourself, 'I need to go to the gym, I need to go to the gym, I need to go to the gym', but you never made it to the gym?

You might say that you're not disciplined enough to go to the gym, right?

Wrong.

You are 100% disciplined in NOT GOING to the gym.

It's not your discipline that's at stake here; it's your HABIT of not going to the gym.

Change your habit from not going to the gym to going to the gym, and you will now be 100% disciplined in going to the gym.

You are 100% disciplined at everything you do or don't do in life.

If you want a different result, change your habits.

Discipline is not about forcing yourself to do something.

It's about creating new habits that inspire you to do something.

Change your habits.

FALLING SHORT

In GOLF:

A short putt will have zero chance of making it in the hole.

FALLING SHORT

In LIFE:

You are capable of more than you think.

Take whatever you think you are capable of, and then add that little bit of extra to it.

This will help you go beyond your comfort zone.

The real excitement in life exists outside your comfort zone.

Look at a baby that reaches the toddler stage. They get there by naturally going beyond their comfort zone.

You were born to keep doing this.

Don't fall short.

Fall forward.

POOR START

In GOLF:

It happens—your first tee shot results in a blowout score on the first hole.

It's not the end. It's just the beginning.

POOR START

In LIFE:

A poor start to your day is not a sign of how your day will turn out. It's simply a poor start.

There is NO connection to how your day started and how your day will finish unless you choose to carry the emotions of your start with you all day.

Your day is a series of events, with a new beginning for each and every event.

What a wonderful way to enjoy a day, no matter what happens within it.

It doesn't matter how you start. What matters is what you do in the next moment.

Create new moments.

HUMBLE

In GOLF:

No matter how well you played that hole, golf has a way of humbling you on the next.

HUMBLE

In LIFE:

Even when you're having an unbelievably great day, stay humble and grounded, as great moments never last either.

Stay humble.

EXPECTATIONS

In GOLF:

Having the expectation of an outcome is the one sure way to destroy the joy of your round.

Imagine expecting every shot you make to go as planned.

Statistics show that rarely does a professional golfer's ball go where they intended it to go.

Professional golfers miss the fairway and the greens around 40% of the time.

Yet they can still win without meeting their expectations.

Golf is a game of progress, not a game of expectations.

EXPECTATIONS

In LIFE:

Expectations put you on edge.

Expectations make you tense and rigid, and life is not supposed to be tense and rigid.

By all means, have a goal, have a vision, but also open yourself to achieving it in different ways, even those you didn't anticipate.

Sometimes, not getting what you expected can be a great thing. It can open you up to new opportunities.

Start your day with a mind open to different possibilities and outcomes.

Have the expectation of no expectations, and see what happens.

THE JOURNEY

In GOLF:

There is nothing quite like hitting a pure shot… the way it sounds, the way it feels, is magic!

Making a 'pure shot' is rare.

To be able to make a pure shot, shot after shot is extraordinarily rare.

Imagine the journey you would have to go through in order to be able to put together a string of those magical moments round after round!

THE JOURNEY

In LIFE:

There are two components to success.

The journey and the end result.

The end result doesn't happen without the journey.

The journey is longer than the end result.

Don't wait for the end result in order to celebrate.

Celebrate your milestones so that you stay motivated and connected to the end result.

Cheers to your journey.

HONESTY

In GOLF:

You've probably played with someone who you know cheats.

Some are so good at cheating that you're not even aware of it.

But who's cheating who here?

HONESTY

In LIFE:

The worst win in life is a win you achieved through cheating.

Being dishonest may go unnoticed by others.

But in the end, you will always know and feel the truth, no matter how you justify it.

The truth will weigh on you so deeply that no gain will ever be satisfying for you.

Being honest is winning.

RIGHT APPROACH

In GOLF:

Imagine a dog-leg left hole with water on the right and bunkers on the left.

There is going to be a landing area on the fairway, which will give you the right approach onto the green.

Anything outside of this landing area will only increase your chances of getting into trouble.

RIGHT APPROACH

In LIFE:

There are multiple ways to solve a problem.

There is always a common problem-solving approach that offers you a much higher chance of success if you follow it.

Success leaves clues.

When others have succeeded before you, they have left you a proven pathway to follow.

Follow it.

SKILLS

In GOLF:

You can go out and buy the most expensive driver in the world, but that alone won't be enough to make you a great driver of the ball.

SKILLS

In LIFE:

Skills, skills, skills… you will be greatly rewarded for your skills!

What makes you skilful?

It's the combination of two things: knowledge (know-how) and intelligence.

Seek out the right people to give you the right knowledge about the skill you want to learn.

Apply and grow your intelligence level around this knowledge, then watch your skill grow exponentially.

People are always looking to attract skilful people to help them solve problems.

Be that person.

IMPLEMENTATION

In GOLF:

You can invest hours and hours watching videos about how to chip out of the rough.

Every golf coach has their own idea of what's best.

There are as many chipping ideas as there are chipping videos.

So, which idea is right for you?

There's only one way to find out:

Implement!

IMPLEMENTATION

In LIFE:

Ideas are everywhere, even genius ideas, but most are just that— ideas.

What's the point of having an amazing idea if you're not going to implement it?

For some people, coming up with ideas makes them feel smart or semi-productive because, deep down, they know they're not going to do anything about them.

They will get praised by their peers for the idea, and that's enough for them.

There are two kinds of people: the idea creator and the idea implementer.

They need each other.

If you're great at creating ideas but not doing anything with them, then team up with a highly-skilled implementor and vice versa.

Or be both.

PERCEPTION

In GOLF:

Have you ever noticed that when you look back at the tee-box from the back of the green, the hole looks very different?

The fairway slope looks different.

The total distance looks different, even shorter than it looked from the tee-box perspective.

The degree of difficulty looks different, yet it's the same hole!

What's changed?

Nothing except your view-point, your perception of the hole.

PERCEPTION

In LIFE:

Everything you see is guided by your perception of how you see things.

Two people can look at the same situation, but each will see it in a different way.

So, who's viewpoint is correct?

Both are correct… it's all perception.

Seek other people's perceptions of the problem you are trying to solve.

Their viewpoint may be better than yours.

Be perceptive.

TIRED

In GOLF:

It's late in your round, and you're getting tired—both physically and mentally.

You start to make 'care-less' decisions.

Everyone notices your change in attitude.

You are not being the normal you.

You spiral, and your score card is not pretty.

TIRED

In LIFE:

It's normal to get tired. It's not normal to always feel tired, so address that now.

Whether you're running a family, a business, your job, or just yourself, remember this:

Never make important decisions when you're mentally and physically tired.

It sounds simple enough, but most people make impulsive, kneejerk reactive decisions that fail them.

Sleep on it.

Then, act on it.

NERVES

In GOLF:

You're standing over a 3-foot putt for the biggest win of your golfing career.

Your heart rate increases as you think about the moment.

Everyone's looking at you from the outside.

You're looking at yourself, even more intensely, from the inside.

Your nerves take over. Your hands, neck, and shoulders all tense up.

And then…? (I'll leave the outcome to your imagination.)

NERVES

In LIFE:

There are going to be moments in your life that will put you on edge.

How you react in those moments will make a huge difference to the outcome.

Your thoughts about the outcome of the moment will trigger your nerves.

Switch from focusing on the outcome to actioning the next step in the process of handling your situation.

Focus on the next step, the next step, and the next step.

The outcome will handle itself.

What nerves?

WORK & LIFE

In GOLF:

If you're a golfing pro, it's too easy to lose sight of the bigger picture.

Golf is the game of your life. It's not your life.

WORK & LIFE

In LIFE:

Games are games.

Life is life.

Don't confuse the two.

STUCK

In GOLF:

There will be periods in your game where you will feel stuck.

Stuck on your handicap level.

Stuck on your average putts per round.

Stuck on your fairways hit in regulation number.

Stuck on your greens hit in regulation number.

STUCK

In LIFE:

You've heard the saying, 'stuck in a rut'.

When everything becomes routine and normalised, it is easy to fall into a rut and feel stuck.

So, what creates routine?

Your habits create routine.

Change your habits, and your routine will change.

When you change your routine, you will experience a new level of excitement and achievement.

Get unstuck.

INFORMATION

In GOLF:

To play great golf, you will need information.

Gathering information means to become 'informed'.

Coaches and caddies can inform you. They can be invaluable to your game.

Choose them wisely, for they will alter your game for better or for worse.

INFORMATION

In LIFE:

There is a great human desire within us to know things before acting.

To learn things is to become 'informed'.

Your deep desire to know things before acting is both your greatest strength and your greatest weakness.

You need information before doing something (your strength), but you may feel you never have enough information, so you don't do anything (your weakness).

So, how much information is enough before acting on something?

The reality is that you will NEVER have 100% of the information you need to make a perfect decision.

So, what's the solution?

Aim for progress, not perfection.

EFFORTLESS

In GOLF:

Have you ever noticed when you hit a pure shot, the club feels like it's an actual part of your body?

The whole event feels effortless, and the result puts a skip in your step on the way to your next shot.

But when you hit a bad shot, your whole-body, jars and you end up increasing the amount of work you'll have to do on your next shot.

EFFORTLESS

In LIFE:

Success doesn't come from putting in a lot of 'hard' effort. It comes from putting in the right effort.

What is the right effort?

Firstly, determine the outcome you want.

Secondly, know what skills / people / tools you will need to help you achieve that outcome.

Take action, and keep in mind: aim for progress, not perfection.

Do this, and your results will feel 'effort-less'.

Become 'effort-less'.

HARD VS. SOLID

In GOLF:

Just imagine hitting a 'hard' shot.

And now imagine hitting a 'solid' shot.

Which one goes further?

Hitting the ball solidly reaps far bigger rewards than trying to hit the ball hard.

HARD VS. SOLID

In LIFE:

You've probably been told that you will need to work 'hard' if you want to get ahead in life.

Forget about doing things the hard way.

Focus instead on working the 'solid' way.

Hard = stressful effort.

Solid = calm effort.

In the long run, solid work will reap far bigger rewards than hard work, both financially and emotionally.

Become solid.

EFFICIENT VS. EFFECTIVE

In GOLF:

What's better, an effective or an efficient swing?

An effective swing is a swing that gives you the result you want.

An efficient swing is simply that: efficient. It has nothing to do with creating a great result.

You can be very efficient at doing the wrong thing.

Check that swing of yours again.

EFFICIENT VS. EFFECTIVE

In LIFE:

Look for ways to be effective in what you do, to have an 'effect'.

Also look for ways to be more efficient, to 'put in less effort'.

When you are both efficient and effective, you have reached the holy grail of producing results.

Be both.

RESILIENCE

In GOLF:

Play golf long enough, and you'll quickly learn that it doesn't take much to get into trouble on any hole.

This is why one of the most exciting times of watching a tournament is witnessing the comeback of a player who is leading, gets into trouble, and then recovers to hold on and win.

RESILIENCE

In LIFE:

We all love a resilience story, a comeback story.

The ability to bounce back is within us all.

To bounce back, start by taking a deep breath.

Inhale deeply and sharply, then exhale slowly for a few breaths.

Now, visualise the outcome you want.

Begin your step-by-step process of taking solid action towards that outcome.

And remember: you have been recovering from undesirable situations since you were born.

You are naturally resilient.

GRATEFUL

In GOLF:

What a glorious game golf is.

No two courses are the same.

There is so much variety to the landscape.

All your senses are stimulated by playing it.

It will test your physical, emotional, and spiritual strength.

It's truly magical.

GRATEFUL

In LIFE:

There is beauty everywhere, if you look for it.

When you don't see it, you have taken this beauty for granted.

So much is going right for you right now.

There will always be moments when things are not going the way you want.

This is not the time to forget how fortunate you are.

To be grateful, stop taking things for granted.

Think gratefully, act gratefully, live gratefully, and all your struggles will fade away.

Be grateful.

TAKING IT FOR GRANTED

In GOLF:

Week in, week out, you show up to the course and play another round of golf.

Do you give much, if any, thought to the work and the effort that goes into maintaining a course in the condition you expect?

TAKING IT FOR GRANTED

In LIFE:

Your problems are relative to everything else being right in your life.

Imagine that today is the day that:

You cannot hear anymore.

You cannot see anymore.

You cannot feel anymore.

You cannot walk anymore.

Before worrying too much about the things not right in your life, be mindful of everything that is effortlessly going right.

Now, what were you worrying about?

TWO WORDS

In GOLF:

Too often, a golfer falls into an internal or external rage after hitting a bad shot.

TWO WORDS

In LIFE:

It's going to happen to you.

You're going to do something that will result in a less-than-desirable outcome.

You have choices regarding how you are going to react.

Try these two words as your go-to reaction: get better.

BALANCE

In GOLF:

A balanced swing is poetry in motion, so many moving parts all working together like a mechanical watch.

Without balance, everything goes out of whack in your game.

BALANCE

In LIFE:

Working too much in one area of your life will always put you out of balance.

Working too little in one area of your life will always put you out of balance.

Balance is about not doing too much or too little.

Look at your health balance.

Look at your wealth balance.

Look at your relationship balance.

Not too much, not too little.

SEIZE THE MOMENT

In GOLF:

As a golfer, you know how to seize the moment.

There are 365 days in a typical year.

There are far fewer golfing days in a year.

This is why, despite gloomy weather, any aches or pains, you will still find a way to show up for a game.

SEIZE THE MOMENT

In LIFE:

Look at the year ahead, and you will see 12 months.

Look at 12 months, and you will see 4 quarters.

Look at 1 quarter, and you will see 3 months.

Look at 1 month, and you will see 4 weeks.

Look at 1 week, and you will see 7 days.

Look at 1 day, and you will see 24 hours.

Look at 1 hour, and you will see 60 minutes.

Look at 1 minute, and you will see 60 seconds.

Look at 1 second, and then it's all gone.

You will reach a certain point in your life where the number of seconds left are less than the number of seconds you have lived.

Seize those seconds.

ANXIETY

In GOLF:

As much as you use your large muscle groups to produce a powerful swing, it's the micro muscles that ultimately determine how you strike or putt the ball.

Those micro muscles are heavily influenced by your feelings.

Nowhere is anxiety more obvious than in a pressure putt situation.

In moments of pressure, tightness and overthinking can become your worst enemies.

ANXIETY

In LIFE:

Anxiety is based around your desire for things to go a certain way or a fear of them not going a certain way.

Either way, anxiety is heavily grounded in your expectations.

Drop your expectations, and you instantly drop your anxiety levels.

When you drop your anxiety levels, you free yourself up for being relaxed, calm, solid, and confident.

Take a deep breath and remind yourself to trust, let go, and enjoy.

After that, whatever happens, happens.

PERSISTENCE

In GOLF:

The game of golf is played over a few hours.

By nature, it is a game of perseverance, a game of persistence—stroke after stroke, putt after putt, hole after hole.

It might seem repetitive to you, but it's not.

Each stroke, each putt, requires a small change here and there.

What can't change is your persistence, your perseverance.

PERSISTENCE

In LIFE:

Life itself is played over hundreds of thousands of hours.

There will be many ups and downs, many successes and failures.

Persistence is a must if you want to achieve anything of value.

Give up the wrong things.

Persist with the right things.

When you persist with the right thoughts and the right actions, the results will take care of themselves.

Success is never final, and complacency is a trap.

No matter how well you are doing, it's crucial to keep moving forward and striving for improvement.

Keep it constant and consistent.

SELF-INTEREST

In GOLF:

Are your playing partners really interested in the way you played your round today?

What they're actually interested in is how well they played their round.

Ultimately, golfers are focused on their own journey, not yours.

SELF-INTEREST

In LIFE:

Amidst the noise of the world, everyone is tuned into one radio station:

WII-FM—What's In It For Me.

It's a reminder that while you are focused on your own success, others are interested in theirs.

If you really want to help someone, do it in a way that gives them a WII-FM benefit.

There are many WII-FM benefits:

WII-FM Socially?

WII-FM Financially?

WII-FM Physically?

WII-FM Emotionally?

Tune in.

ACCEPTANCE

In GOLF:

'How on earth did that putt not go in?'

You go into brief denial, 'No-way!'

You walk away shaking your head.

ACCEPTANCE

In LIFE:

What is done is done.

It is known as the past because it has PASSED.

You can't undo a bad situation or a poor result.

Your PAST has GONE. It is UNCHANGEABLE.

But you can acknowledge it, learn from it, and use it to progress forward.

Be accepting to move forward.

THE CADDIE

In GOLF:

On the surface, they seem to only be there to carry your bag, clean your equipment, and provide you with course knowledge.

But deep down, caddies are much, much, more than that.

They are your golf coach, your sports psychologist, your strategist, and your companion.

They're there to help you assess but, more importantly, to see the things you don't see—your blind spots. They have wisdom.

They're there to protect you from 'stuff' so that you can be your absolute best by focusing on what you are unique at.

They can be your everything.

THE CADDIE

In LIFE:

You need that one person who is always by your side to help guide you in assessing situations, to help you see the things you don't see.

That one person always has your best interest at heart.

They are not jealous of your success. Your success is their success.

They are there to help you grow from your losses.

They are there to help you celebrate your wins.

Stop pushing your own cart, and free yourself up to only do what you are unique at.

Caddie up.

STUFF-LESS

In GOLF:

Both the physical and the mental stuff are required to play a great round of golf.

There is a rule limit to the number of clubs you can have in your bag, and that's a good thing.

It forces you to limit your 'stuff'.

But there is no limit to the amount of mental stuff you can bring to your game.

And that can be a bad thing.

STUFF-LESS

In LIFE:

You are capable of endless thoughts and feelings.

Some of them will help you, but most of them will not.

You really don't need much to do well.

There is a lot of physical and mental clutter around and within you.

Your mind can only successfully focus on one thing at a time.

Eliminate the physical and mental stuff in your life that holds you back.

Make physical and mental space so that you can focus your time and energy on the things that really matter.

Become as 'stuff-less' as possible.

PROBLEMS

In GOLF:

One way to look at the game of golf is to see it as a game of problem solving.

You have 18 holes of problem solving ahead of you.

You need to assess each hole for all the potential problem areas.

Then, you need to create a quick action plan on how to get there in the least number of shots.

It's easier said than done, and that's why it's so addictive.

PROBLEMS

In LIFE:

When you take on something new, assess the potential problems.

It's easy to get swept up in the beauty of the newness of something, whether it be an investment, a relationship, a holiday, etc.

Seek advice from others who have been through what you are about to go through.

If you are skilled enough, you will avoid or escape the problems relatively easily.

If you aren't skilled enough, it will cost you, but, you will still get through it.

Be a problem solver.

RELIABLE

In GOLF:

Ryder Cup captains need trusted players on their teams.

They need players they can rely on.

A reliable player gives the team confidence, especially under high-pressure moments.

What makes a player reliable?

They have developed a repeatable pattern that they can trust under any circumstances.

Repeatable patterns are golden… you can bank on them.

RELIABLE

In LIFE:

When you become a person that people can rely on, you become highly valuable.

In business, there is a lot that can go wrong in a single day.

And when this happens, who do the business owners turn to fix things?

The reliable ones.

How do you become reliable?

Here are the 3 basics of reliable people:
1. They show up on time.
2. They bring with them everything that is needed for results.
3. They do what they say they will do… zero excuses.

Ultimately, a reliable person is someone who is constant and consistent in the application of their behavior over a very long period of time.

Are you reliable? Are you bankable?

IT IS WRITTEN

In GOLF:

You must keep score in order to play in a competition.

You don't draw pictures on 'how' you played. You write down the number of strokes you took to complete the hole.

Nothing more, nothing less.

If you don't record it, or if you record it incorrectly, you will be disqualified.

That's how important it is to write things down (correctly).

IT IS WRITTEN

In LIFE:

Writing things down seems to be a lost art.

It's almost as if it's not cool to do it anymore.

In reality, nothing is cooler than being 'that person' who remembers what needs to be done and by what time.

If I gave you a list of 10 things to remember by heart, under pressure, you would only remember around 3 to 4 of them.

That's a 60% to 70% failure rate.

Write them down, and you'll have 100% success.

Writing things down does 3 impactful things for you:

1. You will see exactly what needs to be done.
2. You will see when it needs to be done.
3. It will free up your mind to work on other things.

Write it down, get it done, and become a person of high value.

CURIOSITY

In GOLF:

If you ever get the chance to have a conversation with a world-class golfer, there is one thing you will notice (and be impressed by) about them:

They are highly curious.

Despite devoting their entire life to the game, they remain forever curious.

They want to know how to play better, even when they are at the top of their game.

CURIOSITY

In LIFE:

The more you know about something, the more you want to know about that something.

Why?

You succeeded at something because you learnt about it.

You associated succeeding with learning.

Then, you realised the more you know, the more you don't know.

And that keeps you learning, hungry for more.

Learners want to learn.

A know-it-all really doesn't know anything.

Stay curious.

VALUE

In GOLF:

Certain golf courses give you great value.

Others, you'd rather never go back to.

Certain golf coaches give you great value.

Others, you'd rather never go back to.

VALUE

In LIFE:

In economic terms, value is benefit divided by cost.

The greater the benefit, the greater the value.

But economics is not what makes things happen.

People do.

Let's look at psychological value instead of economic value.

Value is not the price you pay but the feeling you are left with after the experience.

In psychological terms, value is 'perceived' benefit divided by cost.

If the perceived benefit of the activity is higher than the cost of doing it, you will want it again.

You will most likely tell others about it.

If you want to expand in your business, in your career, or in your relationships, focus on expanding the perceived benefits you provide over the cost.

Become valuable to others.

REFLECTION

In GOLF:

Whether you played a great or not so great round, there is always value in reflecting on what occurred.

When you reflect over your round, you are giving yourself feedback.

It's through feedback that you get the opportunity to improve.

REFLECTION

In LIFE:

It's too easy to take things for granted.

Days flow into weeks, weeks into years, and years into a lifetime.

But what about pausing for a moment?

Take a still moment to reflect before moving forward again.

Many desire to have an extraordinary life, but the reality is that when you look back at everything, it's the ordinary moments which are truly extraordinary.

Be extraordinarily reflective.

INDECISIVE

In GOLF:

You can't be indecisive in golf.

It's an all-in game.

You have to be all-in on your strategy, your club selection, and your physical and emotional commitment.

This is a game of fractions.

If you are a fraction out of step with your commitment, you will be miles out with your result.

INDECISIVE

In LIFE:

If you had no options, you would never be indecisive.

In some ways, life would be simple, but simple is not always fulfilling.

How about we simplify things AND make them fulfilling at the same time?

Options make you think, and when you think, your fears and doubts creep in.

You can limit those fears and doubts by asking yourself two simplifying questions:

1. What outcome do I want here?
2. What resources do I have that will help me get there in the most effective way?

After this, it's all about being committed to taking action.

The best way to be 100% committed is to not think about any other options.

When you're all-in, there is no room for second thoughts.

Chose and commit.

WINS VS. LOSSES

In GOLF:

Fact: You are going to lose more competitions than you are going to win.

If you expect otherwise, you don't understand golf.

But here's the beauty about golf:

As an amateur, you can lose a competition but still lower your handicap.

That's a win.

As a pro golfer, you can lose a competition but still walk away richer.

That's a win.

WINS VS. LOSSES

In LIFE:

There is no life competition.

You don't win or lose at life.

You progress through it.

You have a unique progress journey.

Everyone around you has their own progress journey.

Don't compare your journey with someone else's.

You have no idea what they have gone through to be where they are.

When you progress, you are winning.

When things are not going your way, change the way you progress.

Progress is not a straight line.

Love your progress journey.

YOUR ACTIONS

In GOLF:

Observe any local club golf competition, and you'll quickly notice how quiet it is.

There are no crowds, no cheering, just four people quietly hitting a small round ball for a few hours.

But it is during those few hours of play that you can really notice the character of a person.

It's said that the Japanese love to play golf with you before they sign off on your business deal.

Your true character is easily revealed in a game of golf.

You might appear as a very calm and relaxed person, but then you shank the golf ball into the bushes.

You instantly react in that moment, you can't help yourself, it's an automatic knee-jerk reaction.

Your actions have now revealed your true character.

I'm sure you've partnered up with someone, and by the end of the round, you said, 'I'd hate to do business with that guy!'

YOUR ACTIONS

In LIFE:

Don't listen to what people say. Watch what they do.

Actions speak louder than words.

THE SHOP FRONT

In GOLF:

A winning golfer is not always a winning golfer.

You can win on the outside but be in absolute turmoil on the inside.

THE SHOP FRONT

In LIFE:

Imagine if you expressed exactly how you felt on a daily basis.

I dare say you'd quickly become a person that others would want to avoid.

So, what do you do?

You put up a shop front, a disguise so that you can get along with others.

We all do it to some extent.

Social media is a perfect avenue for this disguise… be wary of this powerful shop front.

Share what's behind your shop front to those you trust.

Unburden yourself.

You might be surprised how light you will feel and how your energy levels lift to progress through life with a bit more joy, a bit more passion.

The shop front is just that… a front. What's happening behind the scenes is your reality.

Address your reality.

ADAPT

In GOLF:

The game of golf is a game of adaptation.

Every shot you take requires you to adapt to the situation you are in.

You adapt your club choice, your strategy, your stance, and your swing.

You do this for every shot, for every hole, over and over again.

Those who can adapt the most intelligently are the winners.

ADAPT

In LIFE:

Your today will not be the same as your yesterday.

Everything is changing around you and within you.

Your body, your emotions, your relationships, your finances, your health, your feelings, your confidence, your fears and doubts… everything is in constant change.

With constant change, you have a daily choice.

Adapt to the change now or become a casualty to the change tomorrow.

A life well-lived happens for those who adapt the fastest to an ever-changing environment.

Be adaptive.

UNEXPECTED

In GOLF:

You wouldn't want to bank on anything in a game of golf.

There is so much that can go wrong or right in an instant.

No matter how well you read the greens, sometimes they will break in a way that you didn't expect, resulting in a 3 putt and an end to your tournament.

UNEXPECTED

In LIFE:

Unexpected things will happen to you.

Don't be too surprised.

The weather does unexpected things. You adapt, and life goes on.

Life throws you a curve ball. You adapt, and life goes on.

Most of your life will be predictable.

There will be moments where this won't be the case.

They are just moments, not your whole life.

An unexpected event in your life can be the change you needed.

It will wake you up from the predictable pattern you have fallen into.

It can be an opportunity for a better path.

Expect the unexpected.

OVERWHELM

In GOLF:

Imagine if you had to drive, chip, and putt all at the same time.

How would you play?

How would you handle it physically?

How would you handle it emotionally?

It's a ridiculous idea because it would put you into complete overwhelm.

You'd have too much to deal with, and it would produce a terrible score.

You play better golf with a single club, with a single focus.

OVERWHELM

In LIFE:

There will be times when you will find yourself bombarded with things.

When your mind is racing, take a blank sheet of paper and write down all your thoughts and feelings in bullet points.

By doing this, you are making the invisible visible.

Writing things down is a very powerful step, both visually and emotionally.

Now, tackle one single item on that list with one single focused action.

You can action some of those items on your own.

For some, you will need help from others.

Others can do some for you.

Single action – single focus.

Doing less is your key to success.

IN THE NOW

In GOLF:

It's impossible for you to play well unless you are totally in the now.

Try putting the ball while thinking about your finances.

Try driving the ball while worrying about your relationships.

To play exceptional golf, you will need to be exceptional at blocking ALL distractions.

IN THE NOW

In LIFE:

You think there is a past, but there isn't. There's only a memory of it.

You think there is a future, but there isn't. There's only a thought of it.

You think there is a now, and there is. You're experiencing it right now.

Every second of your life is a 'now' moment.

No past, no future.

Amazingly, you get to create a new life, a new start with every new moment.

You don't have a past or a future, just a now.

So, from now on, put all your energy, all your focus on the one thing in front of you.

Whether it be about kids, home, work, or friends, do not worry about the past or the future. Give yourself your now energy, and watch things excel for you.

Imagine what you can achieve, who you'll become, when you give everything you've got to your 'now moment'.

You are in the now.

BEHAVIOR

In GOLF:

Does your behavior on the golf course affect everyone on the golf course?

No, it doesn't.

Your behavior really only affects the group you are playing with.

Beyond that, your behavior has little effect on the rest of the playing field unless you're on the big screen.

BEHAVIOR

In LIFE:

What you do does not affect everyone.

You can switch on the news and watch a disastrous event unfold from the other side of the world. Within minutes, you will most likely forget all about it.

But, if that disastrous event actually happened on your street, the effect of that news would be completely different.

Behaviors that are close by are felt very differently from distant behaviors.

Your behavior won't affect the whole world, but it will affect those who are closest to you.

How much of an effect you have is determined by how much you have disrupted their journey.

Engage in positive, uplifting behavior with those closest to you.

The alternative is just bad behavior.

UP & DOWN

In GOLF:

Why is it that you can have a great round today but tomorrow is the complete opposite?

Very simply, you and the course are in a constant state of change.

Players who can adapt to this change the quickest have the highest chance of success.

UP & DOWN

In LIFE:

Time has a very powerful effect on you.

Every day, your mind and body will be greatly influenced by 4 factors:

1. What you eat and drink.
2. The environment you live in.
3. The amount of exercise you do.
4. Your friendships.

The above four core factors are always different from day to day, which is why every day is different than the next.

Make these four factors work for you, not against you.

CHANGE

In GOLF:

Minute by minute, hour by hour, the course you are playing is in a constant state of change.

Wind, rain, sun, hail, humidity, atmospheric pressure, and clouds all have an effect on the way you play the game.

These are the uncontrollable factors in your game.

You can't control the uncontrollables!

It's how you react and adapt to the uncontrollables that determines how well you will play.

CHANGE

In LIFE

As much as you would love to control your outcomes, not all things are controllable, just like the weather.

Think about your mind and body for a moment.

Your mind and your body's cells are in a constant state of change.

How you feel and how you think are always in a constant state of change.

Don't expect to have high-success days duplicated day after day.

This also works in the opposite direction.

Don't expect to have low-success days duplicated day after day.

When in the flow, flow.

When things are not flowing, take a breather.

Change is coming.

LIFE

In GOLF:

With every round you play, good things will happen, and not so good things will happen.

At least they are happening.

Good and bad, they make up your round. What a privilege it is just to be able to play.

LIFE

In LIFE:

Imagine a life where you have 100% certainty over the outcome of everything you do.

Think deeply about this.

The beauty of life, what gives it meaning and desire, is the unpredictability of it.

Take the good with the not so good… it's a privilege to experience both.

Life is short. Death is long.

Trust, let go, enjoy.

BEING ON A HIGH

In GOLF:

When your game is on a high, and it will be, absolutely enjoy that moment.

Because it will only be a moment.

I'm not saying that to be negative. I'm just being realistic with you here.

You can't be on a constant high, as that will become your new normal, and your new normal can't be called a high anymore.

Take a look at your last twenty recorded rounds, and you will see what I mean.

Your improvement will happen over time if you practice the right things.

Highs are the spikes on your upward improvement curve.

BEING ON A HIGH

In LIFE:

It's a wonderful feeling to experience a high.

They will come to you in many areas of your life: your family, your relationships, career, money, etc.

But they won't last, and they won't be there every day. Most of your day will be repetitive.

Because of this repetitiveness, the highs will stand out. They give you feedback that you are on the right track.

Celebrate your highs, but more importantly, celebrate your progress.

Progress can be constant.

REMEMBER THE GOOD

In GOLF:

Many top-ranking golfers have a knack for remembering only their good shots.

They develop a short-term memory of the bad and a long-term memory of the good.

This type of viewpoint gives their mind and body a positive feedback loop to keep improving.

REMEMBER THE GOOD

In LIFE:

Imagine if you lived your life only remembering the bad things that happened.

What type of person would you become? All events in your life are feedback events.

They inform you of what worked and what didn't.

Both are great positive feedback events that help navigate your next move in life.

Look for the good, and you'll see more good, both in yourself and in others.

Look for the bad, and you'll see more bad, both in yourself and in others.

Only you can decide what to look for. Make a choice.

COACHES

In GOLF:

Coaches see what you can't see.

You are your own internal eyes and ears for your game improvement.

They are your external eyes and ears for your game improvement.

Both you and your coach are essential for rapid improvement.

COACHES

In LIFE:

There are multiple studies that show car crash witnesses report completely different versions of a crash, even though they witnessed the exact same car crash!

How can this be? Viewpoint.

Everyone has a different viewpoint.

Everyone sees different things about what you are going through.

Seek those who have had success in coming out of the situation you are in right now.

They will see the things that you don't, or even can't, see right now.

You have blind spots.

A great friend will help you become aware of them and the actions you need to take.

Self-coaching will only take you so far.

Seek an external coach, a mentor, or a trusted advisor.

Be coachable.

JUDGEMENT

In GOLF:

The game of golf does not judge. It does not discriminate.

It doesn't care who you are or where you came from. It doesn't care about your goals.

It simply says, 'Here I am. Play me as you wish. Your choices will determine your results!'

JUDGEMENT

In LIFE:

There are two types of people: those who judge and those who get judged.

Don't be either.

There is nothing to judge.

You are here to experience life.

Let yourself and others experience it. Your choices will determine your results.

GOOD LUCK VS. BAD LUCK

In GOLF:

Do you believe in good luck and bad luck, or do you believe that you make your own luck?

Let's see what happens on the course.

You hit a perfect shot on a par 3, your ball is flying right at the green, and then in a split second, your ball hits a tiny stone on the edge of the green and deflects right off into the water.

That's called bad luck.

You did all the right things, but then something outside of your control changed your outcome. It's rare, but it happens.

Equally, maybe you hit a lousy shot. It travelled way off course, hitting a tree and rebounding straight onto the green, rolling into the hole.

That's called good luck.

You did everything wrong, but then something outside of your control changed your outcome. It's rare, but it happens.

GOOD LUCK VS. BAD LUCK

In LIFE:

You don't make your own luck.

There are greater forces outside of your control. Sometimes you get lucky.

Sometimes you get unlucky.

But you have to show up, and you have to be there to take action. The more you show up, the luckier you get.

Show up.

PERCENTAGE

In GOLF:

Imagine this:

You play just one round where you are only allowed to play your highest percentage shot—the shot that gave you the highest chance of success.

Imagine how much better your score could be.

But, I get it. You're human, and there is that little voice in your head that creeps out and tempts you to 'go for the hero shot'.

That's your low percentage shot, and on average, it fails you at least 80% of the time.

If you knew that you would lose at least 80% of the time doing something, would you continue to do it?

High percentage play beats low percentage play every single time.

PERCENTAGE

In LIFE:

When you look at doing something really important, ask yourself: 'Is it highly probable (80%+) that this will work out for me?'

Everything may seem possible, but not everything is highly probable.

Choose highly probable.

THE CUP

In GOLF:

Why do we have a cup on the green? It is the end point of every hole.

The ball must drop into the cup.

This one little thing makes the whole game meaningful.

Who would come and watch a game of golf if there was no end point?

Even more importantly, who would play a game of golf if there was no end point?

Nobody wants to watch people aimlessly walking around, hitting a ball with no end point.

Get the ball into the cup with the least amount of strokes in a tournament, and you will also win the cup.

THE CUP

In LIFE:

Everything you take on needs an end point.

Work out what your end point is for every major goal you set.

It could be a business goal, a personal goal, a financial goal, a spiritual goal, or a physical goal.

Everything needs an end point in order for people to get involved.

People are moved to achieve great things when you give them an end point.

Your life itself has an end point. Use that to inspire you and others.

Set an end point.

RECOVERY

In GOLF:

It's going to happen…

You're going to stuff up a shot on an important hole. There's only one thing left for you to do now: recover.

RECOVERY

In LIFE:

Never has there been a book written where things go perfectly for all the characters.

What a boring story that would be!

The most talked about stories are the stories about recovery.

How did they stuff up? What did they do? What were their fears and doubts? What was their strategy?

It's going to happen. One day, you will stuff up—big time.

What's important at this point is not your stuff up but your recovery.

Stuff up… recover… stuff up… recover… stuff up… recover. Show them what you're made of with your recovery.

Recovery is the spice of life.

UNSURE

In GOLF:

Unlike a standard basketball court, there is no standard golf course.

And that is the beauty of golf—no two courses will ever be the same.

This fact will open you up to being faced with holes you have never faced before.

You're going to feel unsure how to play certain holes.

This is when you need to remember that you don't hit a golf ball with your head.

You hit it with your whole body.

Your head only thinks, and that's part of the solution, but golf requires a whole-body solution.

Your mind and body feel the whole situation.

UNSURE

In LIFE:

When faced with uncertainty, you don't say, 'I think unsure'; you say, 'I feel unsure'.

That's your clue for how to handle any situation. You need to get the feeling right on what to do next. Where does this feeling come from?

It comes from every cell in your body.

It is where your knowledge, your skills, your wisdom, and your perception will all combine to give you a 'gut feeling' for what to do next.

Every cell in your body has intelligence, not just your brain. Be wholly intelligent.

OUTSIDERS

In GOLF:

Outsiders will look at you and think: 'Why a hybrid club, when you're so close to the green?'

You know better than anyone else that at that point it just feels right to do.

OUTSIDERS

In LIFE:

Don't take notice of outsiders who are judging you.

They are not feeling and seeing what you feel and see right then and there.

They don't have the same experience of the situation as you do. There are billions of outsiders but only one of you.

It's far quicker and simpler to take notice of yourself. Commit to and go for what you feel is best for you. Listen to the insider.

LOGIC

In GOLF:

Golf seems to be a game of logic.

You have a set number of clubs to use in a logical way. Every club serves a purpose.

You don't drive with your putter, and you don't putt with your driver.

That's as logical as this game gets.

You don't win this game based on logic.

During a round, your clubs don't change—you do. Your clubs are logical; you are not.

Your mind and body are constantly changing... even during the round, so you can't rely on your logic alone.

It's when you rely solely on logic that you choose the wrong club and stuff up.

Question how your whole body feels about the next shot.

It's your overthinking, your over-logic, that confuses your whole-body feel.

LOGIC

In LIFE:

When faced with making a decision, it is normal to apply logic. But that's not logical.

You are not a machine. You are human.

Go back and ask yourself, 'How does my whole body feel about the decision I'm about to make here?'

If it's more of a thought than a feeling, then you are confusing your feelings.

Don't confuse your gut feeling with over-logic. Ask your mind-body feel.

SAYING SORRY

In GOLF:

If you know you have done something wrong, saying 'sorry' goes a long way.

It calms the emotions of those affected.

It shows that you are aware that your actions have had an effect on your playing group.

It frees you up to continue playing without clogged emotions. You are now free to focus on your next shot.

SAYING SORRY

In LIFE:

You have a greater chance of repairing a relationship just by saying 'sorry'.

It has to be a genuine apology. Otherwise, it can further disrupt the relationship.

How your 'sorry' is taken by others is not in your control. The right thing to do is to give a genuine, heartfelt sorry. Once delivered, move on, even if they choose not to.

WHY AM I DOING THIS?

In GOLF:

This is the game you chose to play.

No one said that you would enjoy this game every single time you play it.

You play it because you choose to play it.

If it's causing you misery, get professional help.

If professional help doesn't work, take a break from it or, ultimately, choose another game.

Everything you do serves a purpose for you. Playing poorly may be serving a purpose for you.

WHY AM I DOING THIS?

In LIFE:

Sometimes you need to ask yourself some big questions, like: 'Why am I in this relationship?'

'Why am I doing this job?'

'Why am I_____(fill in the blank)?'

The simple answer to all of these questions is: you choose to. It serves a purpose for you to continue doing what you do.

Sometimes that purpose has expired.

Sometimes that purpose simply needs reassessing. Or maybe you're just having an off day.

Ultimately, whatever you do, the good needs to outweigh the bad. Otherwise, the bad will destroy you.

Question the purpose.

HIGH RISK - HIGH REWARD?

In GOLF:

There always that one risky shot that, if successful, would be your shot of the day.

It would be the shot you all talk about at the clubhouse—well, at least you'll be talking about it.

The only problem with high-risk shots is that they have the lowest probability of succeeding.

If you have shots to lose, then the risk is reduced. Most of us don't have shots to lose.

HIGH RISK - HIGH REWARD?

In LIFE:

The all or nothing, high risk – high reward attitude has destroyed many relationships.

Winning in life is a slow, hour by hour, day by day activity. Succeeding is a slow, repetitive process.

Don't be fooled by the media.

They only show you the highlights of someone's life. They don't show you the reality.

If you don't have money to lose, don't risk it.

If you have a relationship you want to keep, don't risk it. Many things are possible, but few things are highly probable.

NEGATIVE SPIRAL

In GOLF:

So, you shank your shot into the trees.

It takes you by surprise, but you tell yourself that it happens to the best of us.

You take a provisional ball, and you shank it again.

Your mind starts to race. You ask yourself, 'What is going on here?'

You start to lose confidence and begin to spiral.

NEGATIVE SPIRAL

In LIFE:

Here's the thing about negative actions: your last action is not connected to your next action unless you choose to connect them.

Don't connect them. They have nothing to do with each other. They are 100% separate events.

Don't weaken your mind by connecting separate negative actions.

This will only bring fear, doubt, and lower confidence. Wipe the slate clean in your mind.

Every, and I mean EVERY, action you take is a new action. There is no connection to what you last did.

Stay new.

SERIOUS PEOPLE

In GOLF:

Have you played with a serious golfer before? They have a do or die energy about them.

Maybe this is you?

If so, you're no fun, and it's going to be a very tense, up and down, gloomy round for you and your playing partners.

If being serious was the winning factor, then those who were the most serious would always win, right?

They don't.

SERIOUS PEOPLE

In LIFE:

Being serious only expresses your underlying fear of things going wrong.

It's like you're trying to control your outcomes to achieve perfection.

You can't.

You're still going to get to where you want to go. The only difference will be how much you will enjoy the journey.

Life is not to be controlled. Life is to be experienced.

Experience it with wide-eyed wonder and amazement. Life is long but also very short in the scheme of things. Smile and laugh often at it.

FOCUS

In GOLF:

There are two types of distractions you will need to deal with. Internal: Your mind and body distractions.

External: People and physical environment distractions.

The weather, the condition of the course, the way you feel during your warm up, the nerves on the first tee… they are all distracting you from one thing: your Focus.

FOCUS

In LIFE:

You can simplify your whole life by doing one thing: choose one thing of high value to focus on.

When you focus on that one thing, you automatically unfocus on everything else.

When you unfocus on everything else, you end up giving maximum energy to that one thing that will matter the most.

Unfocus to focus.

UNCONSCIOUS EFFORT

In GOLF:

Your mind, your body, and your club all need to work together as one momentous force.

This will produce what seems like an effortless result.

Make no mistake—you are putting in effort, but it is synchronized effort.

Unsynchronized effort is hard work.

With enough practice, synchronized effort will become unconscious effort.

Unconscious effort will feel 'effort-less'.

UNCONSCIOUS EFFORT

In LIFE:

There is conscious effort—things you are aware of that you do. Breaking a bad habit is a conscious effort.

And then there's unconscious effort—things you are not aware of that you do.

Breathing while you sleep is an unconscious effort.

Unconscious effort is masterfully synchronized. You are not aware of it. It is 'effort-less' and allows you to focus on other things in life.

When you become 'unconsciously competent' at something, like brushing your teeth, it allows you to focus on other, more important things in life.

Put in effort, master it, make it unconscious effort, rinse and repeat.

Be 'effort-less'.

DEALING WITH FAILURE

In GOLF:

It's going to happen.

You just need that one putt to take home the trophy. And you lip the cup.

DEALING WITH FAILURE

In LIFE:

Success doesn't reveal your true character—failure does. Success tells you one thing: repeat what works.

Failure is feedback.

Failure tells you one thing: work on what didn't work.

Reflect on your character during these failure moments, then grow from them.

And most importantly, decide what type of person you want to be when you recover from them.

Failure is not failure; it's feedback.

MONEY

In GOLF:

At a professional playing level, earning money is crucial to your survival in the game.

On a basic level, it puts food on your family's table.

Where you finish on the leaderboard determines how well you and your family will eat.

But you can't play golf with your eyes on the leaderboard.

Focus on your processes, and the leaderboard will take care of itself.

MONEY

In LIFE:

Money is the end result of a process. It requires effort.

It requires movement. It requires thought.

It requires doing.

There is a 'work hard' money myth: the harder you work, the more you will have.

If that were true, then those who work the hardest would have the most.

We all know plenty of people who work hard and yet don't have more.

Who has more, then?

Money flows to those who are able to effectively do three things.

They know how to combine information with their intellect and take action to get rewarded for it.

Make the money flow.

PERSONALITY

In GOLF:

During your next round, observe how your playing partner plays.

Observe their personality. Does it change when they hit a poor shot?

Do they blame themselves? Do they blame others?

Do they learn from it, or do they repeat the mishap? Golf brings out your true personality.

PERSONALITY

In LIFE:

Personality is everything.

Your personality will do one of two things for you.

It will either attract people to you, or it will distance people from you.

The more you can attract people to you, the greater your opportunities in life.

Decide on your personality, for it will decide your success in life.

Be personable.

WORRY

In GOLF:

Have you ever played with a golfer who always looks worried? They make you tense.

They even make you worry, too.

It serves a purpose for them to worry, but it's not an effective purpose.

WORRY

In LIFE:

Worry stems from not being able to control an outcome. Take the weather you're experiencing today.

You can worry about the weather, but you can't control it—which can make you worry even more about it.

Instead of worrying about the weather, combine the information you have about the weather (rain, wind, humidity, UV levels) with your intellect to make the best use of the weather.

You're not trying to control the weather here.

You're working on how to combine the weather facts with your intellect to your advantage.

There's nothing to control, only to make the best use of. Don't worry about worry.

STRESS

In GOLF:

There are three major areas of stress in golf. Physical stress, indicating how your body feels. Emotional stress, indicating how you feel.

Relationship stress, indicating how things are with others. They all affect your game.

STRESS

In LIFE:

Stress is a perception.

You and I can look at the same threat and yet display completely different stress responses.

In your life, you will experience physical, emotional, and relationship threats.

You will have a choice.

You can be excited by the threat.

Or you could stress about the threat.

Threats don't produce your stress levels. Your reaction, your perception of the threat produces the stress levels.

Reword your stress.

UNIQUE TEAMWORK

In GOLF:

You will never achieve anything of significance on your own.

Sure, you might be the driving force, but you won't be the only force.

Elite golfers, whether they know it or not, follow a success pattern.

They are the 'unique talent'.

They surround themselves with 'unique people with unique talent'.

Together, they produce 'unique teamwork'. Unique teamwork produces 'unique results'.

UNIQUE TEAMWORK

In LIFE:

You have a unique talent.

Combine your unique talent with other people's unique talents. This is called unique teamwork.

Unique teamwork will allow you to achieve great things. From this, you will experience great moments in life.

Who will you turn towards to celebrate when this happens? People.

You don't turn to machines or to things.

You look for the people who supported you, who encouraged you, who invested in you.

They are your unique team. Include others in your plans.

Be unique.

DOUBT

In GOLF:

How would you play if you doubted every shot you took? There is no room for doubt.

Doubt comes from feeling uncertain. Uncertainty stems from the fear of commitment. What are you afraid of?

The ball either goes where you want it to or it doesn't. It's that simple.

What makes it difficult is when you attach great importance to where you want the ball to go.

That produces fear, and fear turns into doubt.

DOUBT

In LIFE:

There is no certainty.

There is no one absolute path.

Your world is full of possibilities and probabilities.

You must have full trust, full conviction, when making a choice. Aim for progress, not perfection, in your choices.

Commit to something, or you will fall for anything.

Do not have doubt.

IT IS WHAT IT IS

In GOLF:

An overriding rule of golf is that if you are uncertain of the rules, simply play the ball where it lies.

In other words: don't move it… leave it as it is, and take your shot.

IT IS WHAT IT IS

In LIFE:

Sometimes you may not like the situation you find yourself in. For whatever reason, that is where you have ended up.

There is no use wasting good energy blaming or cursing yourself or others.

Accept your situation, and do your best to get out of it. You might surprise yourself with the outcome.

And remember that this won't be your last shot in life. Accept and move on.

PERFECT TIMING

In GOLF:

The timing of your body movement in a golf swing is crucial to a solid strike.

The timing of your mental thoughts in a golf swing is crucial to a solid strike.

But perfect timing, every single time, of both—now that's as rare as a hole-in-one.

No player has ever won any golf tournament with perfect timing.

PERFECT TIMING

In LIFE:

To time something perfectly is rare—so rare that it's not even worthy of setting it as a goal.

It will be emotionally taxing and a great waste of your time and energy.

You don't need perfect timing to do well in life. Show up, be present, be prepared, and commit fully.

Aim for 'progress timing'.

APPRECIATION

In GOLF:

What a privilege it is to be able to play this amazing game.

So much effort is required to let you play the game—the greens keepers, the club, the landscape, the people.

They are all to be appreciated.

APPRECIATION

In LIFE:

Stop and think for a moment.

What is going right for you right now?

Did you think about your lungs, your nervous system, your circulatory system, your muscles, your tendons, your skin, your vision, your hearing, or your sense of touch?

Or did you think about things outside yourself?

When you have a better understanding of yourself, appreciation will instantly appear.

The instant you take things for granted is the instant you lose appreciation.

Let yourself and others close to you know that you don't take things for granted.

Go as far as to also appreciate the beauty in all the imperfections of yourself and others.

So much is going right for you right now. See it and appreciate it. Your life will be much happier and fuller as a consequence.

Grow your appreciation.

POSITIVE THINKING

In GOLF:

You can be standing on the tee-off box, staring at a skinny fairway with water on the right.

You try to think positively, telling yourself to 'avoid the water'.

You can visualise exactly where you want the ball to land (not in the water).

That's all positive thinking, and on the surface, it seems to be working—up until you take a swing and the last micro-thought is 'don't go in the water!'.

And guess where your ball goes?

The only thing that really matters is your last micro-thought, not all that prior positive thinking.

POSITIVE THINKING

In LIFE:

Don't think of a pink elephant. What did you just visualise?

A pink elephant, right?

Trying to suppress a thought or fear only makes that thought and fear even bigger.

Positive thinking is often a cover up for what you fear or want to avoid.

The key is to acknowledge your fears. Don't suppress them… bring them out into the open.

The instant you acknowledge them is the instant you will free your mind and your energy to focus on the real outcome you're after.

Instead of positive thinking, let your last 'micro-thought' simply be the result you want to see.

Try it. You'll be positively amazed.

PLAY IT FOR ME

In GOLF:

If I am your caddie and you ask me to play your shot for you, you will be disqualified from the tournament.

Golf requires your results to be a reflection of your own efforts.

PLAY IT FOR ME

In LIFE:

I can catch, cook, and feed you fish every day of your life. You will never go hungry—until I can't do it anymore.

You need to learn the skills to sustain yourself.

If you rely on others, if you feel entitled, if you assume privilege, you will crumble the minute you are on your own.

Build your skills, excel with them, and then teach your loved ones to do the same.

Stand on your own two feet.

MOTIVATION

In GOLF:

There are many ways to motivate yourself for today's game. You could listen to your favourite music.

You could read your favourite quote.

But there is only one thing that REALLY motivates, and it's not positive thinking or positive sayings.

It's results!

MOTIVATION

In LIFE:

What happens when your positive thinking doesn't produce the result you want?

You start to question your positive thinking as a source of motivation.

The most sustainable source of motivation is getting a result. Results motivate people!

When you achieve your desired result, your mind and body form concrete emotional and physical bonds that are difficult to break.

Motivate a result.

FAILURE

In GOLF:

To fail is to succeed.

If success in golf is achieving exactly what you want with each and every stroke, then you are going to fail a lot.

But that doesn't mean you won't win.

If all the other players fail more than you do, you win. Golf is a game of limiting your failures.

Start by reframing 'failure' as a success process.

FAILURE

In LIFE:

Things will rarely go your way.

As a consequence, you may feel like you failed. You didn't fail.

You were given feedback, and it was you who framed it as 'failure'.

Next time, take that feedback and ask yourself this one question: how do I use this feedback to keep progressing?

Fail to succeed.

STAYING SMALL

In GOLF:

Why is it that you hover around the same handicap for what seems like forever?

Why can't you massively drop your handicap? What's the limiting belief you have around that?

Are you justifying your handicap by saying to yourself that you don't practice enough, don't get coached enough, or don't have the right clubs?

They are all justifiers, keeping you locked in at your handicap level.

How does it serve you to stay at this level?

STAYING SMALL

In LIFE:

Consciously or subconsciously, you can talk yourself into staying small.

Whether you know it or not, staying small serves a purpose for you.

It maintains the relationships you have around you.

Growing big can result in losing certain friendships, and it will also mean making new ones.

At one point in your life, you didn't have any friendships (parents excluded).

Now, you do.

Stay small or grow big… it's your choice.

Do what serves you best.

NEGATIVE PATTERNS

In GOLF:

You can get into a state of mind where you lose your ability to sink short putts—often referred to as having 'the yips'.

The more short putts you miss, the more you reinforce something is wrong.

The more you reinforce something is wrong, the more short putts you miss.

This turns into anxiety, and anxiety turns into a negative pattern.

The reality is that you haven't lost your ability to sink short putts; you've developed a mind-body pattern of missing short putts.

NEGATIVE PATTERNS

In LIFE:

It doesn't take much to fall into a negative pattern.

Let's say you form a negative mindset about your future.

You wake up and your first thoughts are about all the things that are worrying you.

Do this every day, and you'll end up in a negative pattern of high anxiety.

To end this negative pattern, a new pattern needs to be created. To do this, you will need a daily pattern interrupter.

Playing a game, learning an instrument, doing yoga, going to the gym, these are all pattern interrupters. You can't do them properly without forgetting about your worries.

The simplest, most powerful pattern interrupter is practicing some form of meditation.

When you meditate, you are immediately interrupting your negative pattern of constant worry.

From this, a new, life enhancing pattern will emerge. Patterns are made by you, and they can be broken by you.

SLOW DOWN TO SPEED UP

In GOLF:

In moments of high pressure, everything speeds up—your heart rate, your thoughts, your actions.

'I need to make this drive.'

'I need to make this iron shot.' 'I need to make this chip shot.' 'I need to make this putt.'

Tying your emotions to a need is what places unnecessary performance pressure on you.

Rushed decisions are rarely good ones.

SLOW DOWN TO SPEED UP

In LIFE:

Thinking too much and too fast doesn't sharpen you; it blunts you.

To sharpen up, slow down your mind and your breathing. This puts you in a solid state, mentally and physically.

When you're under high pressure, create a state of wakeful meditation.

And then from this state, do your thing.

THE COMPARISON TRAP

In GOLF:

Wherever there is a leaderboard, there will be comparisons made.

You will see players both above and below your score. Comparing your score to other players is the biggest trap of all. If you're not on top, it will make you feel inadequate.

If you're going to compare anything, compare yourself to yourself.

How many fairways have you hit in regulation compared to yesterday?

When you work on your own comparisons, you are in control of improving them.

Compare you with you.

THE COMPARISON TRAP

In LIFE:

There will always be someone better than you—better financially, better looking, better communicator, better lover, better at business, better physically, better career, better house, car, holidays, clothes… just all round better.

When you compare your life to others, you are only looking at the end result of what they have.

You're not comparing the journey they took to get what they have.

Your journey will NEVER be the same as anyone else's.

When you compare, you are not comparing apples with apples.

Instead of comparing yourself to other people's journeys, start by appreciating your own journey.

Your journey is amazing. It's one of constant progress.

Compare your journey to where you came from, to where you started from, not to others.

The grass may look greener on the other side, but the weeds are the same.

Don't compare what you don't know… it's a trap.

SUPERSTITIONS

In GOLF:

Do you have a lucky ball marker or carry a set number of tees in your right-hand pocket?

Have you ever achieved a great result and linked something you did at the time to the win?

You may have formed a superstitious connection between a result and an activity.

Let's say you shot your lowest score ever (result), and you realised that you used a certain coin as your ball marker all day (activity).

Does this become your lucky charm? Dangerous!

What if you lose your lucky charm? Do you lose your luck?

There is something that causes a result, and then there's something that you associate with the result.

This is known as a 'causal effect' or an 'associative effect'.

Superstitions are believed to be causal when, in fact, they are associative.

The coin ball marker was associated with your great round; it did not cause your great round.

So, you can safely play with a new marker, and it would make no difference in reality—only in your mind.

SUPERSTITIONS

In LIFE:

It's natural and very tempting to connect a result with an activity. That's human nature, but it's not scientific.

Routines are not superstitions.

Routines help you stay highly effective.

Taking a time-efficient route to work is a highly effective routine.

Believing that taking a certain route to work will keep you safe from having an accident is a superstition.

Superstitions enslave you.

Everything that happens to you in your life has no connection to your future unless you want to connect the past events.

Superstitions are the connections you make; they are not grounded in any fact.

Instead, understand that you get a new chance, a new beginning, with every action you take.

Choose freely… live freely.

EXTERNAL ENVIRONMENT

In GOLF:

Minute by minute, the blades of grass on the greens are changing.

This subtle change can have a drastic change on how fast the greens will roll.

Now, imagine a huge downpour of rain mid-way through your round. What happens to the speed of the greens?

Are you perceptive enough to notice the change in your playing environment?

Are you able to adapt quickly to the changing environment?

You may have played well today, but don't expect the same result tomorrow.

Consistency of play is a myth because there is no consistency of environment.

Your ability to adapt to the environment is what you must become consistent at.

EXTERNAL ENVIRONMENT

In LIFE:

The weather, the people, the traffic, everything you watch and listen, to forms part of your external environment that you have very little, if any, control over.

The one thing you have total control over is how you react to your environment.

You can't control the weather, but you can control the way you react to it.

You can't control people, but you can control how you react to them.

The weather and the people (including you) won't be the same as yesterday.

This means that there will be a never-ending need for you to control how you react to daily changes.

Nothing is consistent about you or them.

Everything and everyone is going through a daily symphony of change.

Day to day, your life cannot be and will never be the same as the day before.

Become the best adapter to an ever-changing environment, and you will thrive.

INTERNAL ENVIRONMENT

In GOLF:

The quality of your thinking, feeling, eating, drinking, and sleeping will combine within you to form your internal environment.

These factors will have a profound effect on how well you play. Your internal environment is under your control.

When your internal environment is thriving, only then will you be in great enough shape to handle your external environment and win.

INTERNAL ENVIRONMENT

In LIFE:

The way you experience life is largely determined by the way you feel about life.

Your mind and body assess everything that's going on within you.

The biggest influence on your mind and body is what you eat and drink.

Before you order or consume food or drink, place your hand on your stomach and ask yourself this: 'If I consume this, will I ultimately feel energised or drained afterwards?'

Your answer will be instant and highly accurate.

The right foods and drinks fuel the way you think, feel, and sleep.

You know what's right. Do right.

EMOTIONAL INTELLIGENCE

In GOLF:

You don't have to be a genius to play well, but you do need to be golf smart.

To be golf smart, and to achieve ultimate success, you will need to be both physically and emotionally intelligent.

You cannot be one. You must be both.

There are many physically intelligent golfers who know how to hit any shot.

But most of them have inconsistent results because they lack the right amount of emotional intelligence.

You must be able to self-regulate your feelings and emotions under pressure so that you are unflappable.

EMOTIONAL INTELLIGENCE

In LIFE:

You walk into a room full of people. Can you instantly 'read the room'?

Is there tension? Who are the key people? Is it a safe or dangerous environment?

Do you get a strong vibe about what's going on, or are you clueless?

Being able to read the room often indicates a high level of emotional intelligence.

There are also many other types of 'smarts', such as physical, word, number, music, etc.

All these smarts require 'emotional' intelligence in order to get the most out of them.

Here are some keys to practising emotional intelligence. Control your impulsive behaviors and feelings.

Take responsibility for your actions. Adapt to changing circumstances.

Recognize and understand your own and other people's emotions.

Be smart about your smarts.

PEOPLE CHANGE

In GOLF:

Most of us play with the same golf clubs each time we go out for a hit, so no change there.

Apart from the weather and which course you play, the biggest change you will experience will be who you play with.

Who you are paired up with can either enhance or hinder the way you play.

This is the impact of 'people change' in your game. The right people can add a lot of joy to your round. The wrong people can make your game miserable.

Coping with 'people change' is an important factor in the way you play your game.

If you can choose who you play with, choose wisely as each game is precious and time is ticking.

PEOPLE CHANGE

In LIFE:

Your circumstances are always changing. Sometimes it's a small change.

Sometimes it's a big change.

The most difficult change to cope with is not the loss of 'possessions' but the loss of people.

When someone close to you is no longer there, that empty space needs to be understood and put into perspective.

How did your best friend become your best friend? There was a moment when you never knew each other. There was that moment when you first met.

Then there was that moment when they left your life.

Before your best friend was in your life, your life was different. Now that they are not in your life, your life will be different again.

This change opens up the space and opportunity to meet someone new, just like it did before.

OPINIONS

In GOLF:

If there's anything you're going to hear a lot about in golf, it's opinions.

You'll hear them from your friends, your family, your mentors, and even strangers.

Most of the opinions you'll hear will be from unqualified people.

Avoid advice from someone who is more messed up in their game than you.

And equally, don't ignore golf coaches who are not great golfers. Coaching is a highly specific skillset. Not everyone has the patience and intelligence to coach.

There are many aspects to a winning golfer's game.

You will need opinions (from coaches) on how to hit the ball, how to exercise, how to think, what to eat and drink, etc.

Your job is to be wise enough to know whose opinions you should take on.

These decisions will have the biggest impact on your game.

OPINIONS

In LIFE:

The funny thing about opinions is that they come from two types of people: those who have surface-level knowledge and those who are experts in a specific field.

Even funnier is that the people who are not experts will freely give you their opinion, even when not asked for it.

Whereas experts will only give an opinion when asked. Opinions are there to help you solve a problem.

Seek opinions from those who have successfully solved the problem you are addressing.

That's my opinion.

HAZARDS

In GOLF:

There are hazards everywhere.

They are there to test your physical and mental golf smarts. Water and sand bunkers are your most typical hazards.

Water is the biggest enemy of the two.

Imagine a par three hole with a large body of water next to the green.

You hit your shot off the tee deep and into the water hazard. That's a one stroke penalty.

There is zero sense in complaining about the hazard.

It is you that has made your journey harder, not the hazard.

You chose the wrong action and, as a consequence, strayed from a perfectly visible and clear pathway.

No one or thing is to blame.

Take your medicine and move on from disappointment.

HAZARDS

In LIFE:

Everything you do has an element of risk in it.

There is a risk versus reward factor to everything you do.

The risk is multiplied when there is an obvious hazard attached and you ignore it or downgrade its harm.

You need to weigh the risk of doing something versus the reward you might get from doing it.

Driving a car is normally a safe activity.

Driving a car while drunk is hazardous to your health—as well as to others.

There's a cost, a penalty, to all actions when you get them wrong. Acknowledge the hazard, then avoid it.

And if that is too late, minimise the cost, the penalty, that you will need to get out of the hazard.

Know the hazards. Know the cost. Assess wisely.

TRUE COSTS

In GOLF:

There are many costs to playing this wonderful game.

Golf clubs.

Golf balls.

Lessons.

Clothing.

Coaching.

Course fees.

TRUE COSTS

In LIFE:

Everything you do will cost you something.

Money is the obvious cost.

Also consider the cost of your time, your energy, your values, and your emotions.

If what you're paying is too much for the results you are getting, then it's time to rethink.

Assess the true cost of what you are doing.

SUCCESS

In GOLF:

This game was never meant to be mastered. No one will ever achieve the perfect golf score.

Yet there are multiple successes in every game of golf. Being physically able to play is a success.

Playing with great company is a success. Driving the ball to your target is a success. Sinking a tricky putt is a success.

Getting out of a difficult lie is a success.

Nailing an up and down out of a bunker is a success.

These are the successes you need to appreciate and be grateful for.

Everything else is progress.

SUCCESS

In LIFE:

You will never have a perfect life. No one will.

But you will have a life full of successes.

What might not seem like a success to you can, actually, be a big success.

If you can read these words, you have eyesight success—that's a big success.

But you take eyesight for granted and desire bigger things instead.

Be grateful every day for what is going right in your life.

By all means, think big, play big, achieve big, but put it all into perspective.

You are already achieving big.

Everything else you pursue is a journey of progress that puts your knowledge and intellect to the test.

Progress is your ultimate marker of success. Master the journey, not the result.

ANGER

In GOLF:

If anger is within you, it will definitely come out of you during a game of golf.

All it takes is one poor, unexpected golf swing.

One bad deflection and your suppressed anger will expose itself.

Have you ever played with an angry golfer, someone who loses their temper when things don't go to their plan?

What's the vibe of your playing group when you have a player like that in your group?

Will you play with them again?

Anger spoils the joy and beauty of the game.

When things don't go your way, instead of getting mad, give yourself a cheeky smile.

You and I know that it is a privilege to be able to wake up and play this amazing game today.

Spread good vibes, not angry ones.

ANGER

In LIFE:

Anger rattles the people around you, and it throws you and them of course. It's ugly.

Anger will surface when things don't go the way you want them to go.

Why get angry?

Are you the master of the universe?

Do you really want to control the outcome of everything? After a while, there would be no fun in that either.

Anger is uncontrolled emotional intelligence. It's a lost perspective.

Instead of reacting with anger as your go-to emotion, react with a question.

Ask yourself: what's the lesson in this?

Look for the lesson.

CHOICES

In GOLF:

Mathematically, there are unlimited ways to get the ball on the green.

What's the best way? There is no best way. There is just a way.

You can calculate your best choice based on some key numbers: your distance, wind, humidity, slope numbers.

But ultimately, your best choice will come down to two factors: what you see and what you feel is right for you.

Once you decide on this, commit to it with unwavering belief. One choice, one action. Commit.

CHOICES

In LIFE:

There is no perfect choice.

There are low and high success probability choices. And there are big and small choices.

No doubt, you can handle the small choices easily.

But when it comes to pathway-altering choices, like relationships, career, finances, or health, lean on the wisdom of others.

Ask two other people, and you'll have two additional lifetimes of wisdom helping you make a good choice.

Ask them:

'Have you been in this situation before?

'What would you do if you were in my shoes?' Prior success leaves success pathways.

Don't overthink it.

Once you make a choice, 100% disregard all other choices and blindly commit to your chosen action. See it through with pure conviction.

DEGREE OF DIFFICULTY

In GOLF:

In which scenario will you learn more, playing an easy course or a hard course?

You will learn plenty from both.

Playing a difficult course has the benefit of being able to expose two things about you: the gaps in your physical skills and the gaps in your emotional skills.

Playing golf and enjoying golf are two very different things.

You don't need to play difficult courses if you're content with your current skill level and your enjoyment level.

You do need to play difficult courses if you want to highlight your gaps and improve your game.

Choose your course difficulty. Choose your course enjoyment.

DEGREE OF DIFFICULTY

In LIFE:

You don't need to make things harder for yourself.

If you're already in your happy place, enjoy your happy place. You've earned it.

No one gets to a happy place without first experiencing difficulties.

Easy and difficult go hand in hand.

With enough effort, difficult things will become easy. But don't make easy things difficult.

FOOD SWINGS

In GOLF:

Does it really matter what you eat or drink to play well? 100%, it does.

Your whole body is organic (derived from living cells). The golf course you play on is also organic.

Because both are organic, they are both evolving in structure and form every microsecond.

What you eat and drink will affect how your mind and body see and feel your environment.

How you see and feel will affect the quality of your decisions. As you know, golf is game of millimetres.

It is also a game of uninterrupted focus.

Only you know what foods and liquids will allow you to be at your best.

FOOD SWINGS

In LIFE:

You don't have mood swings. You have food swings.

What you eat will affect your mood. What you drink will affect your mood.

Combine both, and they will greatly affect your mood. Beware of short-term foods and drinks that give you a high. For every high, a low will follow.

The lows last longer than the highs.

When it comes to making decisions: don't make them on a high or a low.

Discover your long-term foods and drinks that put you in the most intelligent state possible.

Food right, mood right.

IMPORTANCE

In GOLF:

How important are you to the game of golf? You are important.

And you are totally unimportant at the same time. All golfers are replaceable.

There will always be someone to take your place. Your importance is only temporary.

Your importance can and will be replaced.

IMPORTANCE

In LIFE:

No matter how significant you are, no matter how valuable you are, your importance is irrelevant.

Your contribution, on the other hand, is everything. People of significance come and go.

Their contribution is what is remembered.

Be a contributor.

WRONG ENVIRONMENT

In GOLF:

There will come a time in your golfing life where you will need to ask yourself some important questions.

Questions like:

'Why am I still putting up with this golf course?'

'Why am I still putting up with the people I play with?'

Think about this: the day will come when you will never be able to play golf again. This will be a sad day for you.

It will be made much sadder when you realise that you've put up with a course and people that just didn't bring any real joy to your game.

Have the courage to make a change.

Change your course; change who you play with. You have a limited number of rounds left.

WRONG ENVIRONMENT

In LIFE:

Avoid environments that bring regrets and sadness. Have you heard of the butterfly story?

One way to catch a butterfly is to use a net.

The other is to create a beautiful garden that effortlessly attracts butterflies to it.

It's on you to create an uplifting environment. This will attract the most amazing people to you. Your environment is everything!

Your environment doesn't only affect you—it affects everyone within it and for generations to come.

You can't change people, but you can change your environment. It's in your hands.

Right the wrong.

REWIRE YOUR BRAIN

In GOLF:

Your brain has a left and right side to it. You play logical golf with your left side. You play creative golf with your right side. You need both sides.

If you're a right-handed player, do some practice using left-handed clubs.

If you're a left-handed player, do some practice using right-handed clubs.

Do something opposite… reverse your routine, warm up in reverse, put on your clothes in reverse order, or put on your shoes in reverse order.

When you do this, you will rewire your brain.

Your brain will start to create fresh, new neural connections and pathways.

You will create more 'roads' for your thoughts and ideas to travel on.

This will keep your golf brain fresh and sharp.

REWIRE YOUR BRAIN

In LIFE:

Chances are that, from the moment you wake up in the morning, you follow a set routine.

Routines mean you don't have to think or plan anything… you just do.

Routines are one of your greatest strengths, but they are also one of your greatest weaknesses.

I bet you brush your teeth without realising you're brushing your teeth.

Let me guess that you turn on the water with your same hand, open the toothpaste in the same way, squeeze out the same amount of toothpaste each time, brush in the same sequence, and rinse the toothbrush in the same way.

Routines don't grow your brain.

For the next 21 days, brush your teeth using your opposite hand. 100% reverse your routine order.

You will fumble. You will brush slower. You will feel awkward. But you will also grow your brain.

Trigger your brain to build new roads, to become excited about life, to wake up to bigger opportunities!

Rewire to refire.

STRENGTHS VS. WEAKNESSES

In GOLF:

Should you play to your strengths or work on your weaknesses?

When you work on one part of your game long enough, your mind and body will become highly skilled at that one thing.

This will become your strength.

Your weakness will be everything else you didn't work on.

If you work on every part of your game in equal measure, then you will not have a strength.

The key is to work on your weaknesses and get them to a minimum acceptable level.

Accept that you have a natural strength. Never ignore it. Build on it. Be known for it—even be feared for it.

STRENGTHS VS. WEAKNESSES

In LIFE:

Everyone is great at something but not everything.

In golf, you can't get someone else to putt for you (if that's your weakness).

But in life, you can delegate your weaknesses to others who see that activity as their strength (and you should).

If you're a great ideas person (your strength), you will most likely be a poor implementer of ideas (your weakness).

This is a positive.

Being able to see a solution and generate ideas is a valuable and unique talent.

Being able to implement an idea is also a valuable and unique talent.

You cannot be talented in everything.

Your key to big success is to combine your unique talent with other people's unique talents to create a unique team.

Unique teams produce unique results.

Stay unique.

THE SMALLEST CLUB

In GOLF:

The money is in the short game.

Championships are won or lost in the short game.

To putt well is a symphony of touch, feeling, insight, creativity, prior know-how, visualization, and trust all coming together at exactly the right time.

Your long clubs get you in the game. Your short clubs complete your game.

Guess which club most amateurs spend their time and money on? You got it: the driver.

Which club wins the game? Your putter.

On a par 72 course, 36 of those 72 strokes are your putts. 50% of your score is in your putting.

The smallest club has the biggest impact on your game.

THE SMALLEST CLUB

In LIFE:

The way you look, the way you speak, the way you come across to other people is your 'driver'—these qualities will get you into the door.

But they won't keep you there.

People want to see results, not just big talk. Results come from doing many little things right.

It's the way you strategize and implement all the small actions of your project that will produce big results.

Small actions, big impact.

BIG REWARDS

In GOLF:

There is a very good reason why professional golfers get rewarded so highly for a win.

They produce results. They draw in the crowds.

The sponsors and fans love them and will pay to be near them. The bottom line is that pros get paid to produce a result.

The bigger the result, the bigger the reward. No result = no worthwhile reward.

Once you build a reputation for producing results, bigger opportunities will come your way.

Success attracts more success.

BIG REWARDS

In LIFE:

Take a look at who you employ, who you are paying to be on your team.

Are they pros or amateurs?

You can't expect world-class results by bringing in a group of amateurs.

If they are amateurs, are you the right coach for them? Do you have the time to skill them up?

Pros cost more than amateurs because you don't have to spend time and money skilling them up.

How much is your time worth?

Pay the pros for the results they produce and watch them produce more results.

Sure, they'll have good weeks and bad weeks, but they also know how to get back in the winner's circle.

Surround them with the support and inspiration to see them through any performance slump, like a great caddie.

Pay for results, not effort.

A FULL MIND

In GOLF:

With a full mind, it is impossible to excel at anything in life.

Imagine you have a straightforward, short putt to make to win the most important championship of your life.

Your mind races with the importance of the occasion.

You picture the glory, the trophy, the speech, the prize, but then your mind also fills up with "what if" scenarios.

What if you miss? What impact will it have on you?

What will your coach, your spouse, your family, and friends think of you if you fail?

A FULL MIND

In LIFE:

An empty mind with only one task to complete is the most powerful mind you could ever have.

Great things are achieved when you have an 'empty plus one thought' mind.

ONE SMALL DIVOT

In GOLF:

A well-struck iron or wedge shot will leave a divot. It's just a divot—no big deal if you don't fill it, right? Let's do some math on that one, simple non-action.

Let's say you produce 30 divots in a round.

There are 4 players—that's 120 divots / group / round.

If there are 50 groups playing, that's 6,000 divots per day.

6,000 divots per day multiplied by 7 days equals 42,000 divots per week, or 2.184 million divots per year.

Small actions multiply to produce huge effects. A divot is an injury to the course.

It needs to be repaired on the spot in order to make the spot playable for the next player behind you.

You may not notice, but others are noticing you. Do the right thing.

One small, caring action has a huge ripple effect.

Pay it forward.

ONE SMALL DIVOT

In LIFE:

You entered the world with it being in a certain condition. The big question is, how will you leave?

You don't have to change the entire world, just your world. Every action or non-action taken by you has a ripple effect. It's always the small actions that have big impacts.

If your relationship is not right, take a small action. If your income is not right, take a small action.

If your health is not right, take a small action.

If you did damage to someone, take a small action. These small actions are the start of the repair.

They are transformative, and they are impactful.

Be impactful.

TECHNICAL VS. STRATEGIC

In GOLF:

Who's better—a golfer who is very technical or a golfer who is very strategic?

It depends on who you ask.

Ask a technical golfer, and they'll say a technical golfer. Ask a strategic golfer, and they'll say a strategic golfer.

Luckily, they will both agree that the goal is to get the ball in the hole with the least number of strokes.

There is no value in being a great technician with a poor strategy. There is no value in being a great strategist with poor technique. You need to be both.

TECHNICAL VS. STRATEGIC

In LIFE:

There are technical people in this world, and there are strategic ones.

Unlike golf, life doesn't require you to be both.

When given a problem to solve, here's how the technician and strategist handle it:

The technician asks, 'How can I solve the problem?'

The strategist asks, 'Who can help me solve the problem?' See the big difference?

One works IN the problem, the other ON the problem.

The key here is to reach out to others to help you solve your problems.

The world is full of 'how' thinkers; it's 'how' school taught you to be.

The world needs more 'who' thinkers.

Who, not how.

THE LAST ROUND

In GOLF and In LIFE

There will be a last round for you, both in golf and in life. It will come around quicker than expected.

Imagine the time has come for you to say goodbye to life. You're lying there, realizing that this is your last moment.

Everything you have been through, worried about, or enjoyed will come down to this one last breath, one last thought.

In that moment, what do you want your last word to be?

Now, take that one word and do whatever it takes to move heaven and earth to make sure it is the word you wanted.

You only get so many rounds in life.

If you could have it all over again, what would you worry less about? What would you do more of?

Your immediate answer is what you need to do right now.

Golf is a mirror of life.

It's not easy, but it's beautiful.

Hats off to all of my past,
present and future golfing friends

I hope this book has inspired you
to live an even bigger and better life

- George Bakrnchev

www.ingramcontent.com/pod-product-compliance
Lightning Source LLC
Chambersburg PA
CBHW032031290426
44110CB00012B/752